Pluck

Pluck

Poems

Adam Hughes

AMERICAN POETS CONTINUUM SERIES NO. 216

BOA EDITIONS, LTD. ▼ ROCHESTER, NY ▼ 2025

First Edition
23 24 25 26 7 6 5 4 3 2 1

Publications by BOA Editions, Ltd.—a nonprofit corporation under section 501 (c) (3) of the United States Internal Revenue Code—are made possible with funds from a variety of sources, including public funds from the Literature Program of the National Endowment for the Arts; the New York State Council on the Arts, a state agency; and the County of Monroe, NY. Private funding sources include the Max and Marian Farash Charitable Foundation; the Mary S. Mulligan Charitable Trust; the Rochester Area Community Foundation; the Ames Amzalak Memorial Trust in memory of Henry Ames, Semon Amzalak, and Dan Amzalak; and contributions from many individuals nationwide. See Colophon on page 109 for special individual acknowledgments. Any use of this publication to "train" generative artificial intelligence (AI) technologies to generate text is expressly prohibited.

Cover Design: Sandy Knight
Cover Art: Alexander Andrews on Unsplash
Interior Design and Composition: Isabella Madeira
BOA Logo: Mirko

BOA Editions books are available electronically through BookShare, an online distributor offering Large-Print, Braille, Multimedia Audio Book, and Dyslexic formats, as well as through e-readers that feature text to speech capabilities.

Cataloging-in-Publication Data is available from the Library of Congress.

BOA Editions, Ltd.
250 North Goodman Street, Suite 306
Rochester, NY 14607
www.boaeditions.org
A. Poulin, Jr., Founder (1938-1996)

Canst thou not minister to a mind diseased, / Pluck from the memory a rooted sorrow, / Raze out the written troubles of the brain…

—Macbeth, Act V, scene iii

"Yet, no matter how deeply I go down into myself, my God is dark, and like a webbing made of a hundred roots that drink in silence."

—Rilke

"I want to be bruised by God."

—Charles Wright

The Lord *saith thus: Behold, that which I have built will I break down, and that which I have planted I will pluck up…*

—Jeremiah 45:4

Contents

III.

IV.

A Praise Chorus:

Of all the things I've ever
accomplished, perhaps the greatest

has been learning to tie my shoes.

When I buy a new pair now

I tie them once and never again,
slipping them onto—no, cramming

my foot into their soft insides
like a freezing man in the wilderness
hollowing out a deer for warmth.

Sometimes the things we learn
are a shell, a refuge, a stillness,

an emptiness
only half-
filled and then only

of reticence.

I.

I am the hero with
ten thousand
enemies—each one offers

their death
to make me great
and brave

and the subject of songs
for future generations—

the fire lights up
their faces and their eyes

glow with
tomorrow's dawn
and they are all

the same—all
unkempt and wild
and unmistakably me

Certainty was my birthright. I emerged from the womb with my hands clasped in prayer. The nurse told my mother that I'd be a preacher and everyone laughed. Except God. God doesn't laugh at jokes he's heard before. I was born into the choir loft, a cross tattooed on my tongue, the words of scripture crowding my blood, my eyes full with a cloud of witnesses. My grandfather was my first pastor, the church my first country, prayer my first language.

To question was to doubt and to doubt was to sin and sin led to hell. Every time I cursed, or masturbated, or lied, I immediately prayed for forgiveness in case I died suddenly, because if I died with unconfessed sin I'd be separated from God forever. No one ever told me that, but I knew it to be true. I was certain of my religion. Certainty was my religion.

My favorite plague was the one with the frogs. What did God do with all the frogs afterward? Where do you stick an amphibian plague after its utility has passed? Did they wash into the sea? Clog the Egyptian toilets? Maybe there was a frog rapture—frogs beaming up to heaven like the good guys in the novels I read.

I never drank or smoked, didn't have sex until my wedding night. I kept the cursing to a minimum—most of the time. Went to Christian college. Became a pastor. I prayed no more fervently than that first prayer emerging from my mother.

I'm counting on you
    like a rosary
        the beads all worn

and my fingers
    indented
        like the first

word of a new
    paragraph
        the roundness

of hallowed thoughts
    and the brokenness
        of sacred votives

and the temple
    prostitutes
        who count

to god
    in waves
        more holy

than the tearing
    of skin
        and sundering—

all the found
    things are dull
        and used

while the shiny
    things were never
        lost

but wouldn't have
been missed
anyway

Take me to the place
where it's safe
to sail, where

the eyes aren't deceived
by the horizon with its
false promises
of intimacy. I won't
go to the cheap
side of the stars,

I want the stripes,
the lash while
tied to the mainsail,
I want to earn
this equator
and know that the waves
are not the sea,

they are only
its skin, the light
hairs on a girl's arm,
while her heart beats
a thousand feet
below, in the unspeakable
depths and the unknowable
darkness and the undeniable
beauty that makes
the waves

be silent
and the sky
a chorus of vacancy,
this holy residence
of humble ecstasy.

My first marriage ended after seven years. She fell in love with someone else and that was that. I had a two-year-old daughter, a church, a very public ending, and a new beginning. Still, God and I were roommates. We passed in the hall occasionally and nodded. I was a good preacher but a poor believer. I didn't question. I ignored. Silence is easier to hear than doubt. I got my first tattoo after my divorce. Around my wrist: *Poet Warrior Priest.*

I didn't take the ending of that marriage as hard as I should have. In retrospect, it was a relief. I drained my meager retirement funds and used them to spend thousands of dollars on books. They started stacking up around me—in the bed, on the couch, near my bookshelves. Books I never did read, never really thought I'd read, but needed to possess. I bought books on theology, on history, on language, on sports, on random things I saw on Wikipedia. I bought four books on the Zapatista movement. I bought an entire 22-volume collection of the writings of the church fathers—pre-Nicaean, Nicaean, and post-Nicaean. I bought poetry. So much poetry. I did not find God.

I found sex. I had been looking for that since my marriage. I dated a girl—a single mom, the daughter of one of my employees at the time. We never went on a single date. I only went to her apartment where we watched movies and had sex. It was the arrangement we both wanted and for a while it worked. Yet, sometimes in bed with her, I whispered the Jesus Prayer—*Lord, Jesus Christ, Son of God, have mercy on me, a sinner.* It was very quiet, a breath only half exhaled, but it covered the sound of blood, the ocean in seashells, the thunder of distant locusts. She didn't know the words, their meaning; if she even noticed, she thought I was whispering pleasure and passion; didn't know why I shook my head as if that was part of some terrible ritual, this liturgy of breaking into pieces—holy, fallen, and undefined.

I'd spend the night there on Saturday nights, get up Sunday morning and drive to my church and preach. I didn't find God because I wasn't looking for him. I was looking for me but I didn't find him either.

Beside this unlit fire,
this unadorned altar,
        beneath a sky so clear

it could be leviathan's eye,
this night is a warm hand
        in which to hide

and I exhale
thankfulness
        seasoned with sea.

I like when you speak to me
in a stage whisper,
        enough that I can hear you

while still intimate,
although I know
        you're only doing it for me.

everything
a coup
of light

when I wish
for darkness
I am

illuminated
when I wish
for light

I am
shaded
when I want

to sleep
beyond color
I open

my eyes
to God
and words

spoken into
abyss
—let—

II.

peace is a siege
of herons
perched above
the stillness

waiting to break
the surface

for nothing
is more
peaceful

than the moment
right before
the peace
is shattered

One failed marriage is fine. After two, people begin to wonder. I married my second wife quickly—we'd known each other three months when we got engaged, another three months and we were married. She lived in Virginia, I lived in Ohio. When she moved to live with me, I think we both realized our mistake.

I stopped pastoring. My new wife pointed out that someone who didn't have a relationship with God really didn't have any business being a pastor.

I was quickly becoming a caricature. I couldn't seem to hold a job. I was lying more, covering my tracks. Spending money. Hiding the candy wrappers and empty bottles of pop. Not living a double life, because that implies that two lives are being lived. I was a ghost in all my lives.

Of course, this can't end well. I earned my exile. We separated for seven months. When we reconciled, she announced she was moving back to Virginia with or without me.

I'm adrift among
the breakers—this cold
the hands
of a faith healer—
words of fire and magma
but palms of condensation
and reptile.
There's a tremble
in the touch,
the strain of a great weight.

I do not want to go to Nineveh.
Somewhere in their war temple
their prophets know
that all the music is in the wrong key.
They'll ask me how to tune it
and I will have to make something up.
These white-feathered birds
clinging to the mast
offer no advice and you
can keep them as well.

We made it six months in Virginia. The spider-silk bond that held us was easily broken. I found myself first in a hotel then in a studio apartment without heat or air conditioning. I was alone, six hours away from my daughter, my family, no friends, only books and something resembling God.

I've never questioned God. I've never been the "why me" type. I know why me. I've been selfish, irresponsible, immature. That's not on some higher deity. That's on the lesser deity of myself. I didn't question God in that small apartment. I wasn't angry with him. I wasn't sure he mattered anymore, but I suspected he still did. I was too scared to abandon him altogether, of course. Without him, what was I?

When my second marriage ended, and when the relationship that followed ended as well, the chorus of voices grew deafening. They were all my voices, sometimes punctuated by my parents, my exes, possibly something higher. My life had been incredibly easy. I'd never fallen without someone there to pick me up—parents, family, spouses. I'd never lacked for support or love or grace. And where had it gotten me? The problem with grace is that it's fundamentally unfair. If we deserve it, it's not grace—it's a reward. If we don't deserve it? Well, I don't know where that leaves us. I used to.

there is no love in the shadow
of this affection I cling

to the branch, thin and hollow
as a slender girl's clavicle

knowing it will snap
but unable to let go and feel

the fall all over again—
the fall worse than the landing

that at least offers the peace
of certainty the death

of speculation—I've rebuilt
this altar so many times

the stones are worn
with the familiarity of my trembling

and time-tired wings,
the grace notes of salt

After I left pastoring, I attended a Vineyard Church in my hometown. It remains the place I feel most spiritually alive and where I've learned the most about God. One Sunday I had made my way toward the front during the music time. I was kneeling on the floor, crying, unsure what was next or where to turn. A friend came up and laid his hand on my back and said to me, "Adam, I feel God has something to say to you. You'll have to forgive me, I don't usually use this kind of language. But God is very clearly saying the words, '*Shit or get off the pot.*'"

I started laughing. Not because it was funny or inappropriate, but because it was so spot on. And then I laughed at the idea of a Divine Being who was so frustrated with my bullshit that they resorted to cursing at me. God certainly wasn't the first to feel that way toward me, and likely wouldn't be the last.

the moon looks
like a cigarette
burn on a thigh

I knew a woman
who had perfect
circles all down

her leg from
a parent's cigarette
a neat line

from groin to knee
some days
I wonder if I can

love—life
is a fire
burning itself

out—a flame
consuming
all the fuel

its living
a quickening
unto death

a communion
with no
remembrance

only the pain
of this is my body
broken

I wonder if I'll remember
my consummation
or simply recognize
the shine of old burns
and the whispered lies
of embers

God, this psalm

won't tune.

The words are pretty, but

the music

is set to the wrong key

a chorus of dissonant vibrations.

God, I'm jealous
of your grace. Not the grace
you give other people—
the grace you give me.
I wanted it last night
when I was feeling bad.
Today it does me no good.

God, Maker-of-no-Mistakes,
Sea-Sender, Grace-Spewer,
All-Seeing, All-Knowing,
and yet somehow still
able to go on being God,

I forgive you
for the foolishness

with which you've forgiven me.

tonight I am
a paraphrase
of myself—

words carefully
constructed
left behind

in favor of ease
swift
passage

of a night
spent sleeping
a dark

flash
and sudden
light

all my words
tumbling
like two falcons

in courtship
a falling
grace—tumult

Some days I wake with a seashell over my mouth like a gas mask, the roar of the sea in my chest, the taste of salt in my ears, a whole panoply of ocean and drift and things we foolishly call voyages, as if we have any control over where our vessel goes. Some days the nameless angel wakes me and I roll over to avoid her stare, so fiercely unsentimental. Beneath me I picture the tides, imagining I can imagine them, carrying me from island to island until one of them becomes what I need it to be. Some days I wake and see myself standing heroically at the helm, chest out, eyes bravely forward, the look on my face the one you give when you know you're being photographed but you want it to seem like you don't.

God, it's easy to believe
from isolation—monastery,
exile, the stomach
of a thousand tomorrows,
leviathan with the sad eyes
of a drowned star—
once on the beach
it's back to uncertainty.

today
I'm writing
my regrets

all my pens
the windpipes
of songbirds

the ink an opus
of the hushed
and the halted

it's not
the broken
promises

I fear

it's the ones
that are kept

that keep
the skin
of my forefinger

smooth
as a prayer

Tonight across the sky the pieces of my life are scattered like the body of a Babylonian god. I cannot reassemble them. They refused to stay where I put them this morning, unruly children running where I tell them not to go. Can you find them all? Some were blown by the draft of the flames, like burned bits of napkins tossed into the fire, rising, rising, sinking, rising, dancing. A waste.

One day I'll learn to hold
lightly, the way your fingers
frame a skipping stone
so that it rolls off
your hand—too tight
and it sinks, tumbling
like an unprepared fledgling,
but just right and it flies,
juking and weaving
through the waters,
a rock defying its rockness
when held well.
Instead, I grasp

like a child holding a kitten
while it scratches my arm
and shits
and its eyes bulge
until it goes still
and spent and dark
from love and adoration.

I can fix this.

Do not weep
          for the vine.

God is jealous
of our jealousy

and the small,
small mandibles

of inchworms can chew
surprisingly fast.

III.

I wonder
if the moth
with the owl-

eyed wings
believes
its own illusion

or if it knows
that deception
is worn

like a mantle
of dust
a washable

epaulet
the sad eyes
of make-believe

in my heart
a church
empty

no one
there to see
that someone

kneels there
sagging
before the altar

sick and hollow
eyed from
the unbearable

weight
of light
the seduction

of the holy
the wild
the promise

of nakedness
and being
known

God, are you
pornography?

Every morning
I wake alone
and the night
before, you were
there. Where did you go

God? You never leave
a note that I can
read, only
flowers dropping petals
and letters
written in cuneiform—

I only know they're
love letters
by the hearts that
dot the hieroglyphs.

Some morning
I'll catch you
climbing down
the fire escape
your jeans
over your shoulder

your eyes promising
to call. I'll wait

and wonder why
I do this to us.
I'm sorry

God, I've gone
and pictured you again
with your clothes
off and in my lust
I've read you

all wrong.

I want to have bigger arms. I want my instinctive reaction to almost every situation to be something other than abject terror. I want to be known perfectly and loved anyway. I want people to stay.

I am unhappy. The kind of unhappy where I have to listen to a different song or else all I'll do is weep in the shower, letting the water run down my head and into my eyes. I hate water in my eyes.

Do you know what kind of unhappiness drives a man, alone in a small bedroom, to contemplate reading Moby Dick? The demons know and shudder.

I know all of my failings like I know this language and I use the knowledge of both to carve my flesh like a plastic surgeon, philologies of dissembling. I am unhappy and I wear that like an amulet to ward off the scourge of hope. Nothing is so dangerous to unease like the tiniest pinch of unreasonable expectation. I should do push-ups tonight but I'm too unhappy with these small arms and their insufficiency. So instead I have another drink and write and dream and sail inside this archipelago of brokenness, avoiding the reefs and wrecks, and one day I'll watch as the sun extinguishes the little votives, the little bonfires, the night's million reminders that it is dark, and all the faded stars will be unhappy in their receding and I will still be unhappy. One morning I'll have better things to miss and smaller fears to overcome and the grass will smell of its recent sacrifice, a pleasing aroma, and in that moment—the subtle rapture of enough.

God, when the lights
are off do you check
the doorknob
to make sure you locked it?

When you close your eyes
do you see all my failures?
Or is everything the ruminants
of your victories
and the greatest hits
of your other creations?

In this hour, when the only
sound is the warming
of this small apartment,
I can feel you, watching

me, alone on my bed
writing indecipherable
words and trying to sketch
the dreams you placed

in my mind some eons
before eons were measured.
I know you're here,
why else would the curtains

flutter and the lamplight
shine in so tenderly
and perfectly that I would
give anything for a kiss,

the warmth of soft lips
and the curve of a hip
and you, God, alone
with me, my tears

drying
and yours
still wet.

In the book of Genesis, a central character is a man named Jacob. Jacob is the son of Isaac, the grandson of Abraham. He is defined early in life as a trickster, a con man, contrasted often with his twin brother, Esau. Esau is straightforward, muscular, and earthy, if a bit dim and unimaginative. Jacob is crafty, shifty, and uses his brain to get what he wants. Jacob is dishonest, ambitious, and enters life grabbing his twin brother's heel and refusing to let go.

After many schemes and setbacks, the story continues with Jacob later in life, disillusioned by his earlier quests for glory and riches. The reader encounters him stripped of his previous bravado, devoid of the certainty of God and man's favor that had defined his early life. Instead he is alone, awaiting the arrival of Esau, fully expecting the heavy retribution of a powerful and wronged brother. Gone is the protection of his family, his wit, and his charm—he's left exposed to the debt he has long outrun.

As Jacob sleeps fitfully in preparation for his brother's—and his brother's army's—arrival in the morning, Jacob is visited by a man. This unannounced visitor begins to wrestle with Jacob. Jacob, a grappler since birth, wrestles back. All night this fight is waged, neither side gaining an advantage. As dawn nears, the unknown assailant finally speaks and tells Jacob to release him. Jacob refuses. At this point, he has realized his opponent is supernatural. Jacob says he'll only let go if he receives a blessing. The grabber is still grabbing.

Then the supernatural cheats. He pokes Jacob in the hip, immediately dislodging it. But he blesses Jacob anyway, offering him a new symbolic name and a promise of protection and favor. The opponent disappears and Jacob is left with a promise and a limp. His brother arrives soon thereafter with forgiveness rather than vengeance and the Jacob story moves on to his son Joseph.

Jacob's early certainty had been bruised well before the wrestling match. It had been broken by life. It was in the wrestling that certainty gave way to clarity. Certainty is not found in nature.

Clarity is seeing things for what they are—and more importantly—what they could be.

suppose this is it
God
suppose

this is all I will
ever amount to

would that be enough

there is a certain
berry-ness
to this sticky
sweetness

on my tongue but there
are no berries only briars

and blood

and if
you can crown yourself
with both why
can't I

when will I
fail into
terrible glory

last night I asked
where you were

this morning
you were

a tourniquet

a feather
dipped in tar

an anchor
scraping
the bedsheets

disguised as fingernails
opening my back

you lingered

as salt
and bone
and ash

your legend

several inches
to a mile

In Switzerland it's illegal to own one guinea pig. You must always own at least two. I keep thinking of an illegal Swiss guinea pig, alone and sad, her owner fully believing that he is enough to fulfill all her longings but unable to understand what it feels like to have teeth that never stop growing. If I had a ship, the figurehead would be a guinea pig. Always looking for another guinea pig. My ship would be the best ship because it would always be lonely.

God, can you tell me
how to get this
                                        blood
off my hands?

When I rinse them
in the stream
the waters regurgitate

my sin and the banks
cry accusations
that I already believe
and do not need
to be reminded of.

God, once my hands
were clean—you held
them in yours
while we walked
and discussed the things
before knowledge.

Now, I have to find
you, like a weak signal,
holding my hands
aloft and seeking
higher ground.

how far
is far enough
from you

with your telescopic
with your peering
through the windows

of my ribs
all of your
dark room

developments
of me
in various

stages of undress
taken from
the derelict

building
across the street
vacant

but not
empty
like the sky

full
of potential
corrugated grey

are you
the eye
of a falcon

hunting
or the eye
of a mother

watching
over
her nest

either way
I am
relentlessly observed

I'm tired of waking in dread of the day,
my stomach wallpapering my bones.
I don't ask for much—only to glimpse
that which I'm not sure I believe in
anymore—like seeing a wisp
of a thylacine or remembering
the name you gave me
when you put me together—
sinew, tendon, timber and sea.

Jacob wrestled with God. God cheated. Jacob won. Out the back door today I saw lintels of spring lifted above the driftwood of winter. Jacob became Israel. He limped his way to Esau. He bowed before his hair-bound brother. Looking out to the south, whispers of misplaced parousia, this damn ephod is too big. Peniel. Embracing God and Esau. I've lost thirty pounds since last spring. I've lost two jobs since last spring. He couldn't find Joseph. My ribs are tattooed with lines by Pound. *"And life slips by like a field mouse not shaking the grass."*

You, God, are a ship
and I an inexperienced
pilot. I try to guide you
through the islands
but you will not
be directed. These
channels are treacherous
and full of hidden rocks
and if you don't
let me steer we will surely
sink. How can you be
so selfish, God? How
can you be so
slow to respond
when I spin the wheel
and offer late
and wordless prayers?

God, what right do I have
to enter your cloud, your all-
enveloping brightness?
What have I earned

besides my own misery?
All the crumbs under
your table remain ungathered.
And yet your heart-

echo pulverizes me
like the waves that gnaw
the shore, enlarging the sea
one tide at a time

with their teeth of salt
and recession. What good
am I when you are all
the good there is?

God, I see you, your
hands shoved deep
in your pockets,
your gaze somewhere

other than here or there,
your lips all thin with
concentration and your
shoes untied. Please stop,

I don't want you
to trip. If you really
care, God, please
look at me and smile

a genuine smile. Not
the one that I see on
the faces of people
who almost know me.

God, can you let yourself
out tonight? I would walk
you to the door, but
these covers are so wet
with the spray
of my sorrow-seas

and these bones
are so heavy, filled
as they are with the weight
of the day and the day
before and worn
skies of tomorrow.

God, do you ever grow tired
of my exhaustion? When
I forget your name
do you take it personally?
Or do you take
my indignities

and spin them into
new glory-thread
to replace the jeans
I've worn for days
unwashed?
I'm sorry God

that I'm always sorry.
I think I saw the corner
of your robe tonight,
and I wanted to clip
it, like David before Saul,
but you were swift

God, and I was full
of ponder and so much
indecision. Your feet
fell heavy, like
my unclean hands
and your steps

lulled me to sleep.
I'll wake full
of apologies
and thirsty
for grace.

How many times, God,
must I give up
before you believe me
and leave me alone?
Tonight I took off
my hope and hung
naked and broken
and I swear I thought
I heard you
whistle. God you know
sad people don't whistle.
When will you leave
me to my silence?

God, if I give you these
bones will you make
them into whistles?
Flutes? Will you take
my body and give it
music? Must I be broken
down in order to sing?
Must my bones be empty
before you fill them
with your breath?

Every morning I lay out the pieces of my life upon this altar and watch for fire to descend. Can I offer myself as a living sacrifice? Can I truly lay still on the altar while the anticipation of burning builds? Can I truly lay down my insecurity? My desire for acceptance and approval from others? My desire for affection to somehow give myself value? My longing for validation from others? My fears of abandonment and rejection? My selfishness and my ambition? My desire for the easy path? I lay these things out this morning, by naming them, by calling them out. I offer them to you to be consumed by your fire and returned to me as something pure, something holy, something you intended rather than them consuming me of their own accord. There's a consummation. I'll be on fire either way—the unholy fire of self-immolation or the holy fire of your purification. Come.

What am I supposed to do
with this, God? Tonight I feel

as useful as a bathtub
full of lima beans. You know
how I feel about lima beans.

Tonight I was motionless
from all the things I cannot do

and yet I heard you
whistling and I understood
the words your breath
was forming, could read
the handwriting of your
eyes that spark like an old

Christmas tree on a bonfire,
all blaze and flamepop.
If you want me to be useless

I will lay myself upon
this altar, your arms already
full of ram and my head
already light with smoke,

and hear you call to me
in a language known only
to the two of us, though I
am far from fluent
and I need you to speak
slower, clearer.

Repeat after me, place
your hand on the chapel
of my chest. I hear you
laugh at me and I am
filled with wonder
like the sky fills
with color at sunrise—
slowly and as if coming out
of a long, dark night.

Do you hear
the troughing of the waves,
the in between

when the waters
are neither high nor low,
only separated
like a child's trembling
hands held wide—

how much do you
love me? This much?

IV.

God, if you are the fire
falling on this over-soaked
altar, and if I am
the bloody butchered
beast upon
the earth-cool
stones, what about me

makes you want
to consume me? What
aroma, raw and recent,
drives your hunger?
When all of me has been

returned to vapor
and soaked into your
pores, when all that's left
are teeth to cast lots

and clatter new
dead languages, will you
then be satisfied?
Or will you hang
your head

and whisper softly
the rains
to clean up
what was left
of the ashes?

Silence is never true
silence. There's always

the hum of thoughts,
the buzz of the earth,
the rocks with their so quiet
crying out, the words

said years ago
still speaking, stretching
on into some
dark-star eternity.

Not-yet sounds
like a night terror
and the settling
of an old foundation.
Two silences

that aren't really silent,
but are singing
their war hymns
to each other,

thrashing beautifully
against one another
in the somber
nearly-quiet air

I only breathe
when I forget
to breathe the real air.

What is left when certainty erodes? I once held all of my beliefs in one hand, my future in the other. I stand now with empty hands after a lifetime of grasping.

To stand empty is a deeply unmooring experience. In late 2020 I contracted Covid. The symptoms were fairly mild, but I have Type 1 Diabetes and the effects landed me in the ICU. I recovered and that was that. Until it wasn't.

I ended up being diagnosed with long Covid, at a time when the condition was still poorly understood. For almost two years I would have chest pains, shortness of breath, heart palpitations, extreme fatigue and joint pain, as well as increased anxiety. When I most needed my lifelong certainty, there was nothing to grasp.

Many nights I would take a bath to ease my joints and be so overcome with anxiety and heart palpitations that I was absolutely certain about only one thing—that I would not see the morning. My mind would fill with images of my wife finding my body, of the shrapnel of my leaving embedding into the lives of my loved ones. It was the hardest thing I've ever lived through.

And I had nothing to turn to because I had started peeling away the layers like an archaeological dig, bypassing the artifacts and bone fragments and ending not in bedrock, but abyss.

God, will you still be there
when I'm surrounded
by other people?
Or will I find you
alone in a back bedroom
eating pop-tarts, checking
your cell phone, waiting
for everyone else to leave?

It looks like it's just
you and me again.
Maybe tonight
I can call you
by your secret name
and I'll let you
tell me mine.
I'm gathering all
the ashes of past
fires to give to you,
can you make them
blaze again? Can you
rain down new sparks
and raise up new heat,
God? Last time I was
with you I saw
someone else I knew
or wanted to know
and I ran off—always
running—and God
I forgot to come back.
I'm here now,
but I confess
I'm not confident
in the completeness
of my attention.
I know you
heard all the prayers
I didn't pray
but meant to. I know
you've heard
all the ones my heart
has stored for future
nights like this when
you and I are alone
again, and I am drinking
and you are listening

and then you are reaching
for my cup and you
take a drink
and hand it back to me.

No more words.

(We both know
that's a lie

but what's a small lie
between friends?)

Sometimes I wish
I could be still
to just listen

without having
to hear
myself. But what

to do when your voice
sounds so much like mine?

My parents worry about me. They always have. I'm an only child, their entire legacy and hope wrapped up in one very fallible human. These days they worry about me being in Virginia. They worry about my diabetes. They worry that I play rugby. They worry, more than anything, about my soul. They don't address this directly, rather through inference and asides. But it's clear. They're worried I've been heathen'd. That I've become an apostate—a word they wouldn't use but a concept they would agree with.

They love me deeply, full-heartedly. They give and they cajole and they guilt and they pray and they tell me about the prayer sometimes. They care. They worry.

I love them dearly and want to ease their worries. But I don't have the words they'd like to hear. That I've returned to what I once appeared to be but never actually was. That I'm coming home physically, spiritually, emotionally.

It's uncomfortable here. In the tension of almost and in between and yet but not yet.

I want you
to write the psalm

God. I want more

than these echoes.
I'm tired

of this thick
heart

you gave me.
When you visit
will you leave

me more than the dust
from mothwings? More

than the cat eyes
staring at invisible gods?

When will I read you
and be gasped into awe?

God, the sky
is threatening
to break
                    into dawn.

Today may I be
pulled through
the waters, like
a hooked trout,

caught and wounded
but feeling the waters
pass through me
faster than ever before

exhilarated
by my captivity
and knowing
that upon release

nothing will ever
be the same.
Release me, God,
          but take your time.

I'm better at knowing than doing, a great learner but a bad student, in my head I'm more accomplished than outside it, and I much prefer having written to writing. But today I fed the cat and put away the dishes. I even folded laundry and made myself dinner. These things are a kind of editing, are they not? The stories we tell ourselves aren't good enough. We think they are because in them we are handsome and strong and we have lots of sex and the walls are always the right color and the light is always perfect for pictures. But the walls have teeth and our hair is made of rice noodles and the neighbors are never as nice as they seem and the moon is a leaking ceiling and the gaps in the shower are video cameras that capture the smallness of our intimacy and the ghosts are real. So tell me new stories tonight. Tell me new heroes and take me to new places. No more make-believe though. I want real. I want her and me and a bed with three blankets and too many pillows and a fireplace that doesn't really exist so forget the fireplace. I want chili on the stove or chicken noodle and I want a big bowl of ice cream and I want children who are happy and bills that are paid and fiction that pales in comparison to the poetry of our living. I sing this sacred song beneath the silent stars and it's my voice, but you are all the notes.

what do I know
of you except
sparks
traces of smoke
the charred remnants
of altarfire

in the cathedral
of my rib cage
prayers
sound small
in the hollow
of an empty sanctuary

what have you
ever brought me
except this
dislocation
inescapable light
and a thousand
unnameable joys

God, in the uterine
darkness of morning,
I wonder what it's like
to be excavated
like an ancient
city, one cobblestone
at a time, each unearthed
inscription giving
a clue to what
was never meant
to be discovered—
only lived.

Orion holds out
a little longer against
the inevitable.
Soon he'll fade
into tomorrow
and I'll be in bed
beneath the vulgarity
of daylight. And

God, what of you?
Do you fade?
I know my colors
are more dull
than when we first met.

Brush the built-up
dirt and expose
me, the details
of the buried,
this edge of a coin
not seen since
it was spent.

The bird whose
egg falls from the nest

goes out and looks for worms
the same as they did the day before—

nature abhors a vacuum
but also sentimentality

.

the heavy dark of being
this impenetrable dullness

.

tomorrow whispers
its breath tickling the ear

yesterday shouts
but from the open window

of a passing car
muffled misheard mistaken

maybe we forget
because memory makes

effigies of our pain
and amulets of our ecstasy

monuments carved in soapsuds
and a thousand brokens

all singing the same song
in different keys our discord

a symphony of stained
hands and strained

voices and eggless birds
with worm-full bellies

The soundtrack in the background of my life is the ongoing, constant vibration of almost. I have too much belief to not believe and not enough belief to believe.

In those dark nights in the bathtub, and many nights since, my mantra has been a phrase in Welsh—*yma o hyd*—still here. I'm still here. My map may be filled with blank spaces and dragons, my periods replaced with questions marks. But we're still here. Wrestling. Leaning sometimes toward certainty, sometimes away.

Always almost.

Every psalm

is an elegy.

Everything

is a psalm.

Onward

Acknowledgments

Thank you to the editors of the journals and anthologies in which these poems first appeared, sometimes in different forms and/or under different original titles:

Cumberland Review: "[what do I know]";
Hobart: "[Certainty was my birthright]," "[My first marriage ended]," "[One failed marriage is fine]," "[We made it six months in Virginia]," "[After I left pastoring]," "[I want to have bigger arms]," "[In the book of Genesis]," "[In Switzerland it's illegal]," "[Every morning I lay out the pieces of my life]," "[My parents worry about me]," "[I'm better at knowing than doing]";
Sixth Finch: "[the moon looks like a cigarette burn]."

A huge thank you to the faculty and students in the Randolph College MFA program, particularly Rigoberto Gonzalez, Kaveh Akbar, Diana Khoi Nguyen, Aviya Kushner, Philip B. Williams, Gary Dop, and so many others who had a hand in refining this work into something resembling coherence.

Thank you to BOA Editions and Peter Conners for having faith in this and putting so much effort into bringing it to life.

To all of those who are struggling, wandering, lost, confused, riddled with doubt, tarped over with anxiety, seeking, hoping, and dreaming—welcome.

To my parents—I know this can't be an easy book to read, but I am always grateful for your love, your patience, and your support even when we don't agree. Thank you.

To my kids, thank you for being willing to accept a flawed dad and stepdad.

Finally, to my wife—thank you for accepting me as I am and for always dreaming with me, even when those dreams are scary and crazy and completely illogical. Thank you for never giving up on me and never allowing me to give up. You are my sun, my moon, and all my stars.

About the Author

Adam Hughes is a poet, writer, teacher, and performer living in Bedford, Virginia. Originally from central Ohio, he received an MFA in Creative Writing from Randolph College. *Pluck* (BOA Editions, 2025) is his fifth full-length poetry collection. In addition to his poetry, he is also the author of *This Is Rugby*, a non-fiction book about American rugby culture.

Adam has been a pastor, a hospice grief coordinator, a college professor, a rugby player, an actor, a director, and is currently a high school English teacher. Most importantly, he is a husband and a father.

BOA Editions, Ltd. American Poets Continuum Series

No. 1 *The Fuhrer Bunker: A Cycle of Poems in Progress*
W. D. Snodgrass

No. 2 *She*
M. L. Rosenthal

No. 3 *Living With Distance*
Ralph J. Mills, Jr.

No. 4 *Not Just Any Death*
Michael Waters

No. 5 *That Was Then: New and Selected Poems*
Isabella Gardner

No. 6 *Things That Happen Where There Aren't Any People*
William Stafford

No. 7 *The Bridge of Change: Poems 1974–1980*
John Logan

No. 8 *Signatures*
Joseph Stroud

No. 9 *People Live Here: Selected Poems 1949–1983*
Louis Simpson

No. 10 *Yin*
Carolyn Kizer

No. 11 *Duhamel: Ideas of Order in Little Canada*
Bill Tremblay

No. 12 *Seeing It Was So*
Anthony Piccione

No. 13 *Hyam Plutzik: The Collected Poems*

No. 14 *Good Woman: Poems and a Memoir 1969–1980*
Lucille Clifton

No. 15 *Next: New Poems*
Lucille Clifton

No. 16 *Roxa: Voices of the Culver Family*
William B. Patrick

No. 17 *John Logan: The Collected Poems*

No. 18 *Isabella Gardner: The Collected Poems*

No. 19 *The Sunken Lightship*
Peter Makuck

No. 20 *The City in Which I Love You*
Li-Young Lee

No. 21 *Quilting: Poems 1987–1990*
Lucille Clifton

No. 22 *John Logan: The Collected Fiction*

No. 23 *Shenandoah and Other Verse Plays*
Delmore Schwartz

No. 24 *Nobody Lives on Arthur Godfrey Boulevard*
Gerald Costanzo

No. 25 *The Book of Names: New and Selected Poems*
Barton Sutter

No. 26 *Each in His Season*
W. D. Snodgrass

No. 27 *Wordworks: Poems Selected and New*
Richard Kostelanetz

No. 28 *What We Carry*
Dorianne Laux

No. 29 *Red Suitcase*
Naomi Shihab Nye

No. 30 *Song*
Brigit Pegeen Kelly

No. 31 *The Fuehrer Bunker: The Complete Cycle*
W. D. Snodgrass

No. 32 *For the Kingdom*
Anthony Piccione

No. 33 *The Quicken Tree*
Bill Knott

No. 34 *These Upraised Hands*
William B. Patrick

No. 35 *Crazy Horse in Stillness*
William Heyen

No. 36 *Quick, Now, Always*
Mark Irwin

No. 37 *I Have Tasted the Apple*
Mary Crow

No. 38 *The Terrible Stories*
Lucille Clifton

No. 39 *The Heat of Arrivals*
Ray Gonzalez

No. 40 *Jimmy & Rita*
Kim Addonizio

No. 41 *Green Ash, Red Maple, Black Gum*
Michael Waters

No. 42 *Against Distance*
Peter Makuck

No. 43 *The Night Path*
Laurie Kutchins

No. 44 *Radiography*
Bruce Bond

No. 45 *At My Ease: Uncollected Poems of the Fifties and Sixties*
David Ignatow

No. 46 *Trillium*
Richard Foerster

No. 47 *Fuel*
Naomi Shihab Nye

No. 48 *Gratitude*
Sam Hamill

No. 49 *Diana, Charles, & the Queen*
William Heyen

No. 50 *Plus Shipping*
Bob Hicok

No. 51 *Cabato Sentora*
Ray Gonzalez

No. 52 *We Didn't Come Here for This*
William B. Patrick

No. 53 *The Vandals*
Alan Michael Parker

No. 54 *To Get Here*
Wendy Mnookin

No. 55 *Living Is What I Wanted: Last Poems*
David Ignatow

No. 56 *Dusty Angel*
Michael Blumenthal

No. 57 *The Tiger Iris*
Joan Swift

No. 58 *White City*
Mark Irwin

No. 59 *Laugh at the End of the World: Collected Comic Poems 1969–1999*
Bill Knott

No. 60 *Blessing the Boats: New and Selected Poems: 1988–2000*
Lucille Clifton

No. 61 *Tell Me*
Kim Addonizio

No. 62 *Smoke*
Dorianne Laux

No. 63 *Parthenopi: New and Selected Poems*
Michael Waters

No. 64 *Rancho Notorious*
Richard Garcia

No. 65 *Jam*
Joe-Anne McLaughlin

No. 66 *A. Poulin, Jr. Selected Poems*
Edited, with an Introduction by Michael Waters

No. 67 *Small Gods of Grief*
Laure-Anne Bosselaar

No. 68 *Book of My Nights*
Li-Young Lee

No. 69 *Tulip Farms and Leper Colonies*
Charles Harper Webb

No. 70 *Double Going*
Richard Foerster

No. 71 *What He Took*
Wendy Mnookin

No. 72 *The Hawk Temple at Tierra Grande*
Ray Gonzalez

No. 73 *Mules of Love*
Ellen Bass

No. 74 *The Guests at the Gate*
Anthony Piccione

No. 75 *Dumb Luck*
Sam Hamill

No. 76 *Love Song with Motor Vehicles*
Alan Michael Parker

No. 77 *Life Watch*
Willis Barnstone

No. 78 *The Owner of the House: New Collected Poems 1940–2001*
Louis Simpson

No. 79 *Is*
Wayne Dodd

No. 80 *Late*
Cecilia Woloch

No. 81 *Precipitates*
Debra Kang Dean

No. 82 *The Orchard*
Brigit Pegeen Kelly

No. 83 *Bright Hunger*
Mark Irwin

No. 84 *Desire Lines: New and Selected Poems*
Lola Haskins

No. 85 *Curious Conduct*
Jeanne Marie Beaumont

No. 86 *Mercy*
Lucille Clifton

No. 87 *Model Homes*
Wayne Koestenbaum

No. 88 *Farewell to the Starlight in Whiskey*
Barton Sutter

No. 89 *Angels for the Burning*
David Mura

No. 90 *The Rooster's Wife*
Russell Edson

No. 91 *American Children*
Jim Simmerman

No. 92 *Postcards from the Interior*
Wyn Cooper

No. 93 *You & Yours*
Naomi Shihab Nye

No. 94 *Consideration of the Guitar: New and Selected Poems 1986–2005*
Ray Gonzalez

No. 95 *Off-Season in the Promised Land*
Peter Makuck

No. 96 *The Hoopoe's Crown*
Jacqueline Osherow

No. 97 *Not for Specialists: New and Selected Poems*
W. D. Snodgrass

No. 98 *Splendor*
Steve Kronen

No. 99 *Woman Crossing a Field*
Deena Linett

No. 100 *The Burning of Troy*
Richard Foerster

No. 101 *Darling Vulgarity*
Michael Waters

No. 102 *The Persistence of Objects*
Richard Garcia

No. 103 *Slope of the Child Everlasting*
Laurie Kutchins

No. 104 *Broken Hallelujahs*
Sean Thomas Dougherty

No. 105 *Peeping Tom's Cabin: Comic Verse 1928–2008*
X. J. Kennedy

No. 106 *Disclamor*
G.C. Waldrep

No. 107 *Encouragement for a Man Falling to His Death*
Christopher Kennedy

No. 108 *Sleeping with Houdini*
Nin Andrews

No. 109 *Nomina*
Karen Volkman

No. 110 *The Fortieth Day*
Kazim Ali

No. 111 *Elephants & Butterflies*
Alan Michael Parker

No. 112 *Voices*
Lucille Clifton

No. 113 *The Moon Makes Its Own Plea*
Wendy Mnookin

No. 114 *The Heaven-Sent Leaf*
Katy Lederer

No. 115 *Struggling Times*
Louis Simpson

No. 116 *And*
Michael Blumenthal

No. 117 *Carpathia*
Cecilia Woloch

No. 118 *Seasons of Lotus, Seasons of Bone*
Matthew Shenoda

No. 119 *Sharp Stars*
Sharon Bryan

No. 120 *Cool Auditor*
Ray Gonzalez

No. 121 *Long Lens: New and Selected Poems*
Peter Makuck

No. 122 *Chaos Is the New Calm*
Wyn Cooper

No. 123 *Diwata*
Barbara Jane Reyes

No. 124 *Burning of the Three Fires*
Jeanne Marie Beaumont

No. 125 *Sasha Sings the Laundry on the Line*
Sean Thomas Dougherty

No. 126 *Your Father on the Train of Ghosts*
G.C. Waldrep and John Gallaher

No. 127 *Ennui Prophet*
Christopher Kennedy

No. 128 *Transfer*
Naomi Shihab Nye

No. 129 *Gospel Night*
Michael Waters

No. 130 *The Hands of Strangers: Poems from the Nursing Home*
Janice N. Harrington

No. 131 *Kingdom Animalia*
Aracelis Girmay

No. 132 *True Faith*
Ira Sadoff

No. 133 *The Reindeer Camps and Other Poems*
Barton Sutter

No. 134 *The Collected Poems of Lucille Clifton: 1965–2010*

No. 135 *To Keep Love Blurry*
Craig Morgan Teicher

No. 136 *Theophobia*
Bruce Beasley

No. 137 *Refuge*
Adrie Kusserow

No. 138 *The Book of Goodbyes*
Jillian Weise

No. 139 *Birth Marks*
Jim Daniels

No. 140 *No Need of Sympathy*
Fleda Brown

No. 141 *There's a Box in the Garage You Can Beat with a Stick*
Michael Teig

No. 142 *The Keys to the Jail*
Keetje Kuipers

No. 143 *All You Ask for Is Longing: New and Selected Poems 1994–2014*
Sean Thomas Dougherty

No. 144 *Copia*
Erika Meitner

No. 145 *The Chair: Prose Poems*
Richard Garcia

No. 146 *In a Landscape*
John Gallaher

No. 147 *Fanny Says*
Nickole Brown

No. 148 *Why God Is a Woman*
Nin Andrews

No. 149 *Testament*
G.C. Waldrep

No. 150 *I'm No Longer Troubled by the Extravagance*
Rick Bursky

No. 151 *Antidote for Night*
Marsha de la O

No. 152 *Beautiful Wall*
Ray Gonzalez

No. 153 *the black maria*
Aracelis Girmay

No. 154 *Celestial Joyride*
Michael Waters

No. 155 *Whereso*
Karen Volkman

No. 156 *The Day's Last Light Reddens the Leaves of the Copper Beech*
Stephen Dobyns

No. 157 *The End of Pink*
Kathryn Nuernberger

No. 158 *Mandatory Evacuation*
Peter Makuck

No. 159 *Primitive: The Art and Life of Horace H. Pippin*
Janice N. Harrington

No. 160 *The Trembling Answers*
Craig Morgan Teicher

No. 161 *Bye-Bye Land*
Christian Barter

No. 162 *Sky Country*
Christine Kitano

No. 163 *All Soul Parts Returned*
Bruce Beasley

No. 164 *The Smoke of Horses*
Charles Rafferty

No. 165 *The Second O of Sorrow*
Sean Thomas Dougherty

No. 166 *Holy Moly Carry Me*
Erika Meitner

No. 167 *Clues from the Animal Kingdom*
Christopher Kennedy

No. 168 *Dresses from the Old Country*
Laura Read

No. 169 *In Country*
Hugh Martin

No. 170 *The Tiny Journalist*
Naomi Shihab Nye

No. 171 *All Its Charms*
Keetje Kuipers

No. 172 *Night Angler*
Geffrey Davis

No. 173 *The Human Half*
Deborah Brown

No. 174 *Cyborg Detective*
Jillian Weise

No. 175 *On the Shores of Welcome Home*
Bruce Weigl

No. 176 *Rue*
Kathryn Nuernberger

No. 177 *Let's Become a Ghost Story*
Rick Bursky

No. 178 *Year of the Dog*
Deborah Paredez

No. 179 *Brand New Spacesuit*
John Gallaher

No. 180 *How to Carry Water: Selected Poems of Lucille Clifton*
Edited, with an Introduction by Aracelis Girmay

No. 181 *Caw*
Michael Waters

No. 182 *Letters to a Young Brown Girl*
Barbara Jane Reyes

No. 183 *Mother Country*
Elana Bell

No. 184 *Welcome to Sonnetville, New Jersey*
Craig Morgan Teicher

No. 185 *I Am Not Trying to Hide My Hungers from the World*
Kendra DeColo

No. 186 *The Naomi Letters*
Rachel Mennies

No. 187 *Tenderness*
Derrick Austin

No. 188 *Ceive*
B.K. Fischer

No. 189 *Diamonds*
Camille Guthrie

No. 190 *A Cluster of Noisy Planets*
Charles Rafferty

No. 191 *Useful Junk*
Erika Meitner

No. 192 *Field Notes from the Flood Zone*
Heather Sellers

No. 193 *A Season in Hell with Rimbaud*
Dustin Pearson

No. 194 *Your Emergency Contact Has Experienced an Emergency*
Chen Chen

No. 195 *A Tinderbox in Three Acts*
Cynthia Dewi Oka

No. 196 *Little Mr. Prose Poem: Selected Poems of Russell Edson*
Edited by Craig Morgan Teicher

No. 197 *The Dug-Up Gun Museum*
Matt Donovan

No. 198 *Four in Hand*
Alicia Mountain

No. 199 *Buffalo Girl*
Jessica Q. Stark

No. 200 *Nomenclatures of Invisibility*
Mahtem Shiferraw

No. 201 *Flare, Corona*
Jeannine Hall Gailey

No. 202 *Death Prefers the Minor Keys*
Sean Thomas Dougherty

No. 203 *Desire Museum*
Danielle Deulen

No. 204 *Transitory*
Subhaga Crystal Bacon

No. 205 *Every Hard Sweetness*
Sheila Carter-Jones

No. 206 *Blue on a Blue Palette*
Lynne Thompson

No. 207 *One Wild Word Away*
Geffrey Davis

No. 208	*The Strange God Who Makes Us*
	Christopher Kennedy
No. 209	*Our Splendid Failure to Do the Impossible*
	Rebecca Lindenberg
No. 210	*Yard Show*
	Janice N. Harrington
No. 211	*The Last Song of the World*
	Joseph Fasano
No. 212	*Lonely Women Make Good Lovers*
	Keetje Kuipers
No. 213	*jump the gun*
	Jennie Malboeuf
No. 214	*Apostle of Desire*
	Bruce Weigl
No. 215	*GREEN OF ALL HEADS*
	Aracelis Girmay
No. 216	*Pluck*
	Adam Hughes

Colophon

BOA Editions, Ltd., a nonprofit publisher
of poetry and other literary works, fosters readership
and appreciation of contemporary literature. By identifying,
cultivating, and publishing both new and established poets
and selecting authors of unique literary talent,
BOA brings high-quality literature to the public.

Support for this effort comes from the sale of its publications,
grant funding, and private donations.

⩔⩔⩔

*The publication of this book is made possible, in part,
by the special support of the following individuals:*

Anonymous (x2)
Ralph Black & Susan Murphy
Angela Bonazinga & Catherine Lewis
Gwen Conners, *in memory of June Baker*
Chris Dahl, *in honor of Chuck Hertrick*
Bonnie Garner
Jacquie & Andy Germanow
James Hale
Grant Holcomb
Nora A. Jones
Joe & Dale Klein
Barbara Lovenheim, *in memory of John Lovenheim*
Joe McElveney
John & Judy Messenger
Daniel M. Meyers, *in honor of J. Shepard Skiff*
Dorrie Parini
Boo Poulin, *in memory of A. Poulin Jr.*
Michael Quattrone
Deborah Ronnen
John H. Schultz
Sue Stewart, *in memory of Steve Raymond*
William Waddell & Linda Rubel